EVERYDAY EVANGELISM FOR TEENS

PURSUING HEARTS, NOT ARGUMENTS

PRESTON PERRY

Lifeway Press®
Brentwood, Tennessee

EDITORIAL TEAM, LIFEWAY ADULTS BIBLE STUDIES

Ross Harvey
Writer

Reid Patton
Senior Editor

Katie Vogel
Assistant Editor

Jon Rodda
Art Director

Tyler Quillet
Managing Editor

Joel Polk
Publisher, Small Group Publishing

John Paul Basham
Director, Adult Ministry Publishing

EDITORIAL TEAM, LIFEWAY STUDENTS BIBLE STUDIES

Kyle Wiltshire
Content Editor

Larkin Witmyer
Production Editor

Shiloh Stufflebeam
Graphic Designer

Karen Daniel
Manager, Small Group Resources

Chuck Peters
Director, Next Gen Publishing

Published by Lifeway Press® • © 2024 Preston Perry
Reprinted Nov. 2025

ISBN 978-1-4300-8277-4 • Item 005845470

Dewey decimal classification: 269.2
Subject headings: EVANGELISTIC WORK \ WITNESSING \ TEENAGERS

To order additional copies of this resource, write to Lifeway Resources Customer Service; 200 Powell Place, Suite 100; Brentwood, TN 37027-7707; fax 615-251-5933; call toll free 800-458-2772; order online at lifeway.com; email orderentry@lifeway.com.

Printed in the United States of America

Student Ministry Publishing • Lifeway Resources
200 Powell Place, Suite 100 • Brentwood, TN 37027-7707

Contents

Preston Perry

Preston Perry is husband to Jackie and father to Eden, Autumn, Sage, and August. He is also a poet, performance artist, teacher, and apologist.

How to Use This Study

This Bible study provides a guided process to help individuals and small groups step into the calling of evangelism. Six weeks of sessions give a biblical framework and practical guidance to help prepare students for effective evangelism. Through the book, we will learn the foundational heart posture, principles, and apologetics necessary to win hearts for the sake of Christ.

GROUP TIME

Regardless of what day of the week your group meets, each session of content begins with the group session. Each group session uses the following format to facilitate simple yet meaningful interaction among students and with God's Word.

START

The group session will begin with an icebreaker and a few questions designed to help you introduce the session's topic and encourage students to engage in the conversation.

WATCH

This page provides notes and blanks to fill in as you watch the video teaching. Codes to access the videos are included with your purchase and can be found at the back of this book.

DISCUSS

This section is the main component of the group session. The questions provided are designed to facilitate group discussion on the session's topic. The goal is to help students better understand God's perspective on evangelism and apply the biblical teaching to their lives.

PERSONAL DAYS

The group time and personal days are paired together to help students grow in their understanding of the topic for each session. Two personal days are provided after each group session along with an evangelistic exercise to help students apply the week's teaching to their evangelistic efforts. With biblical teaching and introspective questions, these days challenge students to grow in their understanding of God's Word and to respond in faith and obedience.

Week 1
EVERYDAY EVANGELIST

Group Time

START

Welcome to week 1 of **Everyday Evangelism**.

Icebreaker: Find a partner and discuss these two questions.

1. **How did you become a follower of Jesus? (If you are not a follower of Jesus, discuss why you've not made the decision to follow Him.)**

2. **What does "evangelist" mean?**

The truth is, most Christians find it difficult to share the gospel with others. It can make us nervous and clam up. We're afraid we won't have the right words—especially if someone starts arguing with us. We're anxious that someone might ask us a question we don't know the answer to. If we aren't careful, we'll let these hesitations keep us from this important job God has given us.

We have to think about sharing the gospel, or evangelism, differently. And that starts with remembering God has called us to be evangelists. The word *evangelist* simply means "a sharer of good news." The gospel is good news but only if people hear it.

If we are willing to engage with God's calling to be a sharer of good news, He is more than willing to empower us through the Holy Spirit to share the gospel with anyone we encounter. If you're willing to be used by God, He will use you. This Bible study has been designed to help you embrace this truth and equip you with practical tools to be the everyday evangelist God has called you to be.

Pause to pray as you begin this study, asking God to give you passion and boldness to embrace your calling as an evangelist.

WATCH

Use this page to take notes and fill in the blanks as you watch video session 1.

1. In ________________ be aware when people shut down. They are shutting down for a ________________.

2. "In order to figure out why she was getting ________________, I had to ask her good ________________."

3. "When I shared my wife's story, I could tell that she felt like she could ____________ to me for the first time in a way that she couldn't before. And I saw her ____________."

4. The first indication of somebody being open to you is when they start asking you ________________.

5. "I've seen evangelists . . . only stick with the '____________.' They never get to the '________.' They never truly see people because they don't ask the right questions."

6. "Once people feel ____________, they will allow you to give the gospel to them."

"Lord, I don't know what to say to this lady. Help me."

"When I found a way to relate to her, she felt seen and she wanted to engage in a conversation with me."

To access the teaching sessions, use the instructions in the back of your Bible study book.

DISCUSS

Use this page to facilitate the group discussion.

All Christians are called to be evangelists because what Jesus has done for us is good news. We should want everyone to know about it. And what Jesus commands us to do, He will give us the grace to carry out with confidence because the God who brought the good news to us will be with us as we share it. Through this study, we will learn how to share the gospel wherever God places us—winning hearts like God has won ours.

Read Matthew 28:18-20. These verses are known as the Great Commission.

1. **What does Jesus tell His disciples to do? What encourages you to be an evangelist from these verses? How have you seen these promises hold true for us today?**

2. **In the past, what has kept you from being an evangelist?**

3. **Do you have relationships with people who have different worldviews than yours? If so, what do they believe?**

Much of what keeps us from being evangelists are the burdens we place on ourselves. When you received the gospel, did you believe as a result of one conversation? In most cases, God uses several people, planting and watering seeds over a period of time, to open our hearts to Him. It usually takes time, multiple conversations, and prayer for someone to come to faith in Jesus. When we share the gospel with someone, even if that person does not receive Jesus in that moment, our conversation will never be pointless. We can trust the Spirit's work in his or her life.

Read 1 Corinthians 3:5-9.

4. **What do these verses reveal about God's process for bringing people to faith in Jesus?**

5. **Your responsibility when it comes to evangelism is planting the seed. God is the One who makes it grow. How does this truth impact your mindset about sharing the gospel with others?**

6. **Read verse 9 again. How are we "God's coworkers"? In what ways are the people with whom we share the gospel "God's field, God's building"?**

If you're concerned about having the right words to say when you share the gospel with someone else, remember you're not alone in your efforts. The Holy Spirit has everything you need for the task. When you obediently give people the gospel, He will empower you. The Great Commission is not dependent upon your communication skills; it is dependent upon the power of God in you. As you step out in faith, God will give you the words, the courage, and the wisdom you need to effectively share the good news.

Read 1 Corinthians 2:1-5.

7. **How does the Holy Spirit empower believers for evangelism?**

8. **Do you currently feel comfortable with the idea of sharing the gospel with others? Why or why not?**

Hopefully, today's teaching and discussion have encouraged you to be an evangelist. If you still have hesitations, don't worry—this is just the beginning! As you dive into your personal study days, continue to engage in discussions with your group and rely on the Holy Spirit throughout this process, and your confidence will continue to grow. God is going to do powerful things through your obedience!

Use this time to pray for one another as you close your time together.

PRAYER REQUESTS

Jesus came near and
said to them,
"All authority has
been given to me in
heaven and on earth.
Go, therefore, and
make disciples of all
nations, baptizing
them in the name of
the Father and of the
Son and of the Holy
Spirit, teaching them
to observe everything
I have commanded you.
And remember, I am
with you always, to
the end of the age."

MATTHEW 28:18-20

Week 1 Everyday Evangelist

PERSONAL DAY 1

Commissioned

All of us who are saved by God's grace have a story. God uses His Spirit, His truth, and His servants to call people to faith in Jesus. In my own life, God used difficult life experiences and the ordinary faithfulness of people like my Aunt Denise and my friend Gary to share the gospel with me. I did not respond immediately, but the seeds that were planted and watered eventually bore fruit. God used their faithfulness to completely change my life.

Take a moment to write out your story below. How did God win your heart? What people or which truths did He use to call you to Himself?

All followers of Jesus are evangelists. In the Holy Spirit, every saint has all that is needed to give the gospel to the community around him or her. God uses all faithful Christians to go and tell the world that we were once blind, but now we can see—and that they can, too, if they will only repent and believe. God doesn't use us because we are some sort of all-star Christian. God uses us in spite of ourselves.

Read 1 Corinthians 1:26-29:

Brothers and sisters, consider your calling: Not many were wise from a human perspective, not many powerful, not many of noble birth. Instead, God has chosen what is foolish in the world to shame the wise, and God has chosen what is weak in the world to shame the strong. God has chosen what is insignificant and despised in the world—what is viewed as nothing—to bring to nothing what is viewed as something, so that no one may boast in his presence.

In what ways are you tempted to see yourself as unqualified for evangelism?

What actually qualifies someone to share the gospel?

God can and wants to use each of us to share the gospel. We do not have to have a certain level of status, education, talent, or wealth to be worthy of this calling. We carry an extraordinary power inside of us through the Holy Spirit. Evangelism is much more about what He is doing through us than what we do. God uses our simple obedience to spread and water gospel seeds. The Spirit brings the fruit.

All we need to become an evangelist is the Spirit's work and Jesus's commission. He has commissioned you just as He did the first disciples.

Read Matthew 28:16-20.

Notice that some of the disciples still had doubts about Jesus's resurrection. Why do you think they were struggling to believe?

Jesus tells us to make disciples of all nations, which means we will encounter people with different beliefs and worldviews. How does Jesus's authority give you confidence in approaching those potentially challenging situations?

The One who has "all authority" (v. 18) is with us always (v. 20). This is the truth we should hold to most tightly as we share the gospel—His calling on our lives is our covering as we step out of our comfort zone and into obedience to His commission.

Read Philippians 2:5-11.

What does it mean that Jesus has "the name that is above every name"?

Why is His authority a necessary part of evangelism?

Because of Jesus's humility, obedience, and perfect sacrifice for our sins, God has given Him supreme authority over everything. Therefore, Jesus not only has the right to give commands, He has the power to ensure His commands are fulfilled. Nothing can stand against Jesus. No person, argument, worldview, or power we encounter can defeat His purposes.

With this highest level of authority, He has commissioned us to go and make disciples of all nations. Because He has this authority, we respect and obey Him. And because He has empowered us with His authority, with His Spirit living in us, we can confidently carry out the mission. This is the unshakable foundation upon which we can build a life of evangelism for the glory of God.

PERSONAL DAY 2

On Apologetics

A common hesitation people have in sharing the gospel is the worry that they won't be able to answer every question people throw at them. Many fear evangelistic conversations will lead to arguments that they won't be able to "win." But the goal of evangelism is to win hearts, not arguments. Before we can have productive conversations about the gospel, we need to cultivate a desire to see people come to faith in Jesus—and desire that more than being right or proving a point.

Of course, many gospel conversations involve talking about our deeply held beliefs. We will inevitably encounter people who have different belief systems and worldviews. And while we must always remain focused on winning hearts, we still have to be prepared to defend our faith—which brings us to apologetics.

Do you currently feel equipped to have conversations about the basic truths of Christianity? Why or why not?

The term *apologetics* may make you think about upper level Bible classes or scholarly debates. Maybe you think that unless you earn a master's degree, you won't be able to effectively engage in apologetics. But you don't have to have a deep theological background or be an accomplished scholar to be able to defend your faith. Apologetics is really about loving the Lord and being willing to tell people about Him.

Read 1 Peter 3:13-17.

Summarize what Peter is saying in these verses. Rewrite them in your own words below.

In these verses, Peter provides vital instruction regarding our attitude when we share the gospel. How we speak to people about our faith matters. How they *feel* during our conversations matters, and our approach to these conversations can either invite others to learn more about Jesus or drive them away from Him.

According to 1 Peter 3:16, what characteristics should mark our conversations about faith?

When people challenge you, do you usually respond with gentleness and respect or defensiveness? Why?

We can defend our faith without being defensive. Preparation is the key. If we are confident in our ability to speak about our faith, we can be calm in the face of opposition. Let's consider some of the opposition you might face as you share the gospel.

Think about the people you know who don't know Jesus. What do they currently believe about God?

What are some common misconceptions people you know have about the Christian faith?

The more we are genuinely curious and seek to understand what the people around us believe, the better we can engage with them on matters of faith. If you feel like God is calling you to reach out to the Muslim student in your class, it would be helpful to familiarize yourself with the Quran and the five pillars of Islam. You don't have to know everything, but if you know the key points of that person's faith, you can go into conversations aware of how his or her beliefs differ with Christianity and study Scripture that addresses those areas in advance.

This kind of preparation allows you to interact with your neighbors without anxiety over where the conversation might go. When you feel ready to defend your faith, if the need arises, you can more easily maintain a gentle and respectful disposition. Think about Jesus and the way He interacted with people who didn't believe. He never puffed out His chest or argued with people who disagreed with Him. He simply spoke the truth with conviction and compassion. His kindness led people to repentance.

God called the apostle Paul, a once-devout Pharisee, to spread the gospel across the Gentile (non-Jewish) world. He encountered foreign cultures and interacted with all kinds of people with a variety of customs—and always remained on mission to help people come to faith in Jesus.

Read his words from 1 Corinthians 9:20-22:

To the Jews I became like a Jew, to win Jews; to those under the law, like one under the law—though I myself am not under the law—to win those under the law. To those who are without the law, like one without the law—though I am not without God's law but under the law of Christ—to win those without the law. To the weak I became weak, in order to win the weak. I have become all things to all people, so that I may by every possible means save some.

"By every possible means." A true evangelist, Paul was constantly looking for ways to connect with people in order to have genuine conversations that allowed him to share the truth about Jesus. That required a genuine interest in people and their beliefs. If you want to "become all things to all people," you have to care and learn about people.

What belief systems or worldviews do you need to learn about so that you can prepare for conversations about the gospel with your friends, fellow students, teammates, and neighbors?

What aspects of Christianity do you feel you need to understand more fully in order to defend your faith?

PERSONAL DAY 3

Evangelistic Exercise

You have spent time thinking about your story, or testimony, throughout this first session. Our testimonies are powerful tools for evangelism because they describe our experience with Jesus, reflecting the ways He has changed our lives. Testimonies are helpful because we can immediately share them with people who have other worldviews, and they can't really be argued with because they are our lived experience—the stories of our lives. Sharing your testimony is a great way to begin an evangelistic conversation with either a stranger or with someone you've known for a while. One way to begin is talking about the way having a relationship with Jesus has blessed your life.

For instance, you might have a friend who is going through a difficult time because of the sudden death of a family member. You may not be sure if your friend follows Jesus, but you can take the opportunity to explain to her that one of the blessings of a relationship with Jesus is that He is near to the brokenhearted and gives supernatural comfort in times of need (see Psalm 34:18).

In what ways has your relationship with Jesus blessed your life? How can you use those experiences to start gospel conversations with others? The following prompts will help you think through some entry points for evangelistic conversations.

As you go through these questions, think of someone you already know personally but whose spiritual beliefs you don't know. Phrase your responses to these questions as if you were having an evangelistic conversation with that person.

What about your life has changed most positively because of Jesus?

What is something you're learning about Jesus?

What struggles have you experienced in your spiritual life?

What has been the most surprising impact that Jesus has had on your life?

Who does God bring to mind to begin sharing with? Trust where the Spirit of God is leading. Write his or her name and a prayer for that person below. Include in your prayer a request for God to give you the courage and an opportunity to talk with this individual about Jesus.

Week 2

LOVE PEOPLE WELL

Group Time

START

Welcome to week 2 of **Everyday Evangelism**. *Briefly discuss the last session and talk about any questions students may have.*

Icebreaker: Discuss these three questions about love together as a group.

1. **What makes you, personally, feel most loved?**

2. **How do you know when someone truly loves you?**

3. **What makes you feel unloved?**

In week 1, we began to learn about evangelism (sharing the gospel with others) and apologetics (defending your faith when others have questions). But it's important to remember this is just the beginning. The goal moving forward in this book is to help normalize these concepts that are often overcomplicated.

But as you prepare to share the gospel with others, you must also consider the condition of your own heart. What is your motivation for evangelism and apologetics? This week, we're going to build our foundation for sharing the gospel on love and honor for God and for people. Evangelism can never become about us. If it does, our efforts will be entirely ineffective.

We can only share the gospel if people are willing to listen to us—and people will only listen if they believe we care about them. Remember the things you said that make you feel loved and how you know when someone loves you. Also, remember what it feels like when you feel unloved. We have to apply those things to our evangelism. Jesus didn't just walk around presenting cold, hard facts. He engaged with people; He asked questions, and He told stories. He spent time with people and made them feel seen and valued. He loved them well. If we really want to reach people and win their hearts for the Lord, we have to love them like Jesus.

Pause to pray, asking God to help you see people like He does.

WATCH

Use this page to take notes and fill in the blanks as you watch video session 2.

1. When you share your faith, you're going to run into people who don't ____________ in the Lord and people who have a different view on ____________.

2. Apologetics starts with honoring Christ in our ______________.

3. "If we give the gospel to somebody in a ____________ _________ and not on a dignifying platter, they didn't reject the gospel, they rejected the way you ________ it to them."

4. What if we think about ___________ before we think about the _____________?

5. Love should be the ________________ for our apologetics.

6. "If your ___________ is ready to give a defense for why you believe what you believe, God can ______ you greatly."

"...but in your hearts regard Christ the Lord as holy, ready at any time to give a defense to anyone who asks you for a reason for the hope that is in you. Yet do this with gentleness and reverence..."
1 Peter 3:15-16a

To access the teaching sessions, use the instructions in the back of your Bible study book.

DISCUSS

Use this page to facilitate the group discussion.

John 3:16 is probably the most famous verse in the Bible. But many people aren't as familiar with John 3:17. It says, "For God did not send his Son into the world to condemn the world, but to save the world through him." Jesus knows and understands us in every way. If anyone had the right to condemn the world, it was the perfect Son of God. But He didn't do that. He came to save the world through His love.

1. **What does it mean to "love people well"?**
2. **How did Jesus love people well during His ministry on earth?**
3. **How have people who have impacted your life spiritually shown you the love of Jesus?**

Read John 4:1-26.

Think about the woman at the well in John 4. Jesus didn't first confront her and accuse her of sin. He went out of His way to interact with her. He gently asked her questions and listened to her responses. Because He truly cared about the woman, He interacted with her in a way that was disarming and made it possible for Him to speak truth to her so that when He did bring up her sin, she would receive it. Jesus's compassion for her changed her life, and she immediately went to tell others about Him. When we love people well, like Jesus does, the fruit of that love will multiply.

4. **Ask your neighbor this question and tell him or her to be honest, "Do I tend to talk more than I listen or vice versa?" Then, allow your neighbor to ask you the same question and, in love, answer it honestly.**
5. **Why is listening, rather than lecturing, disarming to others?**
6. **How can you develop genuine care for people and sincere curiosity about their lives?**

During the last supper, as Jesus prepared the disciples to be sent out, He spoke to them about the importance of love. In John 13:34-35, He said, "I give you a new command: Love one another. Just as I have loved you, you are also to love one another. By this everyone will know that you are my disciples, if you love one another." If we want to truly represent Jesus to others, love must be our defining characteristic.

7. **In what ways can you make your love for people more obvious?**

8. **Of all the ways to show Jesus to the world, why is loving others so important?**

9. **How does loving people well open doors for evangelism?**

Love calls us to see people and meet their needs. And the greatest need every person on earth has is the need for Jesus. Sharing the gospel with others is an act of love. If you let love be your motivation in every evangelistic conversation, you will be able to genuinely connect with others and plant seeds that God will cause to grow.

Use this time to pray for one another as you close your time together.

PRAYER REQUESTS

"I give you a new command: Love one another. Just as I have loved you, you are also to love one another. By this everyone will know that you are my disciples, if you love one another."

JOHN 13:34-35

Week 2 Love People Well

PERSONAL DAY 1

Without Love, We Have Nothing

Love is the core of the gospel message. Jesus's love for us and commitment to God's glory led Him to the cross. We love because Jesus first loved us (1 John 4:19). If we are following in the footsteps of Jesus, then we should also be characterized by love. In 1 Corinthians 13, Paul addresses what real love looks like and helps us understand why it is essential for Christians to communicate love in everything we do.

Read 1 Corinthians 13.

What does preaching the gospel without love look like?

What characteristics of love (vv. 4-7) do you find most difficult to show in your life?

We can't be evangelists or apologists without love. Remember what we talked about last week in 1 Peter 3:15-16, where Peter says, "In your hearts regard Christ the Lord as holy, ready at any time to give a defense to anyone who asks you for a reason for the hope that is in you. Yet do this with gentleness and reverence, keeping a clear conscience." The way we approach people is vital to the success of our evangelistic efforts.

No one wants to have a conversation with a prideful know-it-all. That won't get us far with anyone. In 1 Peter 3:8-9 of the same chapter, Peter exhorts us to be compassionate and humble, to bless others even when we are attacked. Gentleness, reverence, compassion, and humility are all fruit of a loving heart. When we approach someone with this posture, regardless of how the person responds to us, we can have a clear conscience knowing that we have represented Jesus well. When we love people well, Jesus is glorified.

Think of someone in your life that you would like to have a gospel conversation with. How would you begin an exchange about Jesus with this person? Think through some different ways you could start that gospel conversation, and write out a few opening questions or statements below.

Look over what you've written and make sure your practice statements communicate genuine care for that person. You never know how the conversation will go; the individual you talk to may walk away without even remembering what you said. But if you lovingly engage the individual, he or she will at least remember how you made him or her feel. That could leave the door open for another conversation to take place in the future.

You may have had some encounters where someone reacted poorly when you reached out. Those awkward or negative experiences can weaken our courage or make us defensive. But we have to continually cultivate an open and humble heart, willing to lovingly offer the gospel without demanding a particular result.

That's what Jesus did for us. Jesus gave everything He had for us—while being spat on in return. Negative responses to His love didn't stop Him from giving it fully. Even today, He continues to pursue people who have been nothing but hostile to Him. Think about how you lived before you knew Jesus. All of us were in direct opposition to Him—and still, He came to us (see Rom. 5:10). Nothing would stop Jesus from sharing everything He had with us. We should take on this same loving perseverance to bring others to Jesus.

Read Romans 5:6-8.

We were God's enemies and He still sent His Son to die in our place. Why do you think He continues to love us (believers and unbelievers alike), even though we sin and have hostility toward Him?

How do these verses encourage you to continue loving people, even when you are rejected?

What are some ways you can love people who are hard to love?

True evangelism requires a long-term commitment to love. Our love for people must be sincere, keeping us engaged when we'd rather give up. Our love must be patient and kind, willing to walk alongside people as long as it takes. And our love should drive us to continually hope for people and "endure all things" (1 Cor. 13:7)—the way Christ's love has never given up on us.

PERSONAL DAY 2

Loving with Our Whole Lives

Jesus loves us more than anyone ever could. He gave up His life for us—and He's asking us to do the same. Evangelism requires us to give up our lives for others. Giving someone the gospel is far more than a simple conversation. It often involves allowing someone into our homes, our social circles, our hearts, and our everyday lives. This kind of outreach and discipleship involves a cost. It takes time, energy, patience, resources, and prayer. If we truly want to follow in His footsteps, making disciples is costly for us. But in light of eternity, the sacrifice is worth it.

Read Philippians 2:5-8.

In your own words, rewrite below what Jesus did to save us according to these verses:

What needs to change in how you share the gospel with others for you to better show Christ?

Jesus is fully God. He had no reason to leave the heavenly realm other than His love for the Father and for us. He chose to lay aside His glory, take on human form, and make the greatest sacrifice anyone could offer. Being fully man, He endured the lowest possible human experience: He was rejected and beaten, mocked and spit on, shamed and hung on a cross. He was condemned as guilty, even though He was innocent. Not once did He complain. His love for us never wavered. But the Bible tells us that the reward for Jesus was incredible.

Read Philippians 2:9-11.

What does it look like to model a Philippians 2:5-8 kind of service and sacrifice in obedience to Jesus's commands in your own life?

How is Jesus glorified when this kind of loving service becomes part of who we are?

Jesus gave us the blueprint for how to live a sacrificial life that honors God. With humble hearts, in grateful response to what He has done for us, we follow the path of Jesus. We lower ourselves like He did. We count others as more important than ourselves. We think about others more than we think about ourselves. We serve people because we love them. And while we don't serve God for our own gain, Jesus says we will have a great heavenly reward for this life of sacrificial love.

What keeps us from being willing to humble ourselves as Jesus did in order to love others?

How might our service, sacrifice, and obedience make us more effective evangelists?

We cannot find a better model than Jesus. He humbled Himself to love us at the cost of His own life. Taking the gospel to others will always cost us something, whether it's our popularity in the eyes of others, the ability to win an argument, or the time it takes to get to know someone. It always comes with a cost that Jesus's love challenges us to embrace willingly because that's what it means to love people well.

This session is about loving people well. Pay attention to that last word. Loving people generally is easy; loving people well takes sacrifice. What do you need to sacrifice to love people well?

Who could you seek to love well? Write his or her name below and write a prayer that God would grant you favor and access with this individual this week.

PERSONAL DAY 3

Evangelistic Exercise

Spend some time in prayer as you begin this session's evangelistic exercise.

Are you fearful of anything when it comes to evangelism? Record some thoughts below and ask God to give you the courage to overcome them.

In light of the topic of loving people well this week, it's time to consider some practical ways you can infuse love into your evangelistic conversations.

What kinds of questions can you ask that show people you care about them?

How can these questions lead to deeper conversations?

Revisit your conversation starters from personal day 1. Have you used any of them yet? If not, that's okay. The goal is for you to be ready when God provides the opportunity. But there are times when He calls us to pursue that opportunity personally. How can you connect this week with the person you mentioned earlier?

Write down your next steps for connecting and showing love to the person God is prompting you to reach.

After you connect with your person this week, return to this page and record your experience.

How did the conversation go? How do you feel? Where do you think your conversations with this person can go from here?

Take time to pray and thank God for the opportunity to show His love to this person, no matter how the interaction goes.

Week 3

SHOW HOW YOU LIVE

Group Time

START

Welcome to week 3 of **Everyday Evangelism**. *Briefly discuss the last session and talk about any questions students may have.*

Icebreaker: Give every student in the group an index card and a pen. Direct them to write three facts about themselves on the card. When they are done, collect the cards and shuffle them up. Then read the cards one at a time and see if the group can guess who it belongs to.

Building off of last week's study on love, today we'll discuss one of the most loving things we can do in our efforts to bring others to Jesus: invite them into our lives. If we are truly following Jesus, the way we live will reflect the change He has made in our lives. The way we move through the world—the way we love, work, repent, and forgive—is a living testimony of God's power to transform our lives.

In the icebreaker activity, we were able to identify who was who from the three facts written on the cards because we know one another. We have to do the same for people who do not know Jesus. By inviting them to be a part of our lives, we communicate our desire for relationship with them. As our friendship deepens it creates space for more vulnerable conversations and offers us the opportunity to model the Christian life. This may seem like a huge sacrifice in terms of time and effort—and it definitely is—but it's worth it!

Who is a person that modeled following Jesus for you? What have you learned from him or her?

I gave my life to Jesus because a friend was willing to share his life with me. Seeing the way he lived compelled me to surrender everything to God. If you have genuinely been transformed by Jesus, you can help others see Him by showing them your life. Don't discount the power of your living testimony.

Pray before watching the video, asking God to help you be vulnerable and open your life to others.

WATCH

Use this page to take notes and fill in the blanks as you watch video session 3.

1. We should give the ___________ to the lost in a way that will make them be intrigued about our God to the point that they'd be willing to ___________ us.

2. If our apologetics and evangelism doesn't ___________ people into our lives, we have to ask ourselves, "Are we doing it ________?"

3. "If we want to make disciples ______________, sometimes that causes us to open up our __________ to show people how we live."

4. Our evangelism and apologetics should be a __________ so people can come in to see how we _________.

5. "If we follow His __________ and we're faithful to live the way He lived, we will never go ____________."

"Go, therefore, and make disciples of all nations, baptizing them in the name of the Father and of the Son and of the Holy Spirit."
Matthew 28:19

To access the teaching sessions, use the instructions in the back of your Bible study book.

DISCUSS

Use this page to facilitate the group discussion.

Depending on where you are in your own journey with God, the idea of being a disciple maker might feel intimidating. But you don't have to have achieved a certain level of almost-perfection in order for the fruit of the Spirit to be evident in your life. If you are following Jesus, you can reflect His goodness to others, even as you continue to grow and work through mistakes in your own life.

1. **How does the way we live impact others and what they think about Jesus on a deeper level?**

2. **How are you currently feeling about the practice of showing others how you live?**

In my life, God used my friend Gary to speak to my heart. In fact, it was a moment of failure in Gary's life that awakened me to the truth of Jesus. That situation never would have happened if Gary hadn't been willing to bring me into his life. What ended up being an eternity-changing event happened through a moment when Gary was real, owned a mistake he had made, and let me in his life in an authentic way. We can never underestimate what God will do if we open our lives up to others and invite them to spend time with us.

3. **If someone observed the way you live, what would they learn about God through your life?**

4. **What worries you about inviting others into your life?**

5. **What do you want your living testimony to show others about God?**

When people observe your life, they don't need to see perfection to get a glimpse of what Jesus can do. They need to see that your life has been transformed by Jesus. You don't have to figure everything out in advance. You just have to be faithful in your pursuit of God and your love for others.

6. **How can God still be glorified even though we are imperfect?**

7. **How can allowing others to witness your failure and repentance point them to Jesus?**

Read Romans 6:1-4:

What should we say then? Should we continue in sin so that grace may multiply? Absolutely not! How can we who died to sin still live in it? Or are you unaware that all of us who were baptized into Christ Jesus were baptized into his death? Therefore we were buried with him by baptism into death, in order that, just as Christ was raised from the dead by the glory of the Father, so we too may walk in newness of life.

While you don't have to be perfect to show people Jesus, they do need to see evidence of "newness of life" in you. They need to see you actively working to put the old life behind you. We can't continue in sinful habits or neglect our relationship with Jesus and expect others to see Him when we share our lives with them. A life that reveals the goodness of God is a life lived in faithfulness to Him.

8. **In what way can you more faithfully walk with Jesus this week? What impact can that have on people around you?**

Use this time to pray for one another as you close your time together.

PRAYER REQUESTS

"A person should think of us in this way: as servants of Christ and managers of the mysteries of God. In this regard, it is required that managers be found faithful."

1 CORINTHIANS 4:1-2

Week 3 Show How You Live

PERSONAL DAY 1

Faithful in Obedience

Be diligent to present yourself to God as one approved, a worker who doesn't need to be ashamed, correctly teaching the word of truth.
2 TIMOTHY 2:15

In this verse, as Paul encourages Timothy to continue in faithfulness, he says to Timothy, "Keep going. Never give up. Continue sharing what God has shown you in His Word with love and dedication. You will never have to be ashamed, no matter the result. You've done what God has asked."

You can't know in advance how people will respond when you share the gospel with them. You can't predict what God will do in their hearts as you invite them into your life. We don't need guaranteed success in order to be obedient to what God is calling us to do. He's calling us to step outside our comfort zones and offer His life-giving message to lost and hurting people. He calls us to serve them, and He calls us to love them. We can trust that our faithful God is at work in our obedience, no matter what the results appear to be.

In what ways have you been faithful to give people the gospel? In what ways do you need to be more diligent?

Does knowing that God is always faithful encourage you in your efforts to be obedient to the calling He's given you? Why or why not?

In 1 Kings 18, there is a record of one of the most dramatic moments in Scripture. It was a dark time in the nation of Israel; their kings and queens had led the people into idolatry, and they had forgotten God. The current queen, Jezebel, was killing God's prophets, and the prophets who escaped her had gone into hiding. But God raised up the prophet Elijah to bring the people back to Him.

In the presence of all of Israel, Elijah challenged 450 prophets of the false god Baal to a demonstration that would compare the power of their god with the God of Abraham, Isaac, and Jacob. Each side would build an altar with a sacrifice, one for Baal and one for the Lord. Then, they would pray, and the God who answered with fire would be accepted as the one true God. The people agreed, and the battle began.

Elijah was the only prophet of God facing 450 false prophets on the other side, and he threw down the gauntlet. If the God of Israel did not respond with fire, Elijah would most definitely be killed. But he put everything on the line, even at the risk of his life, to bring the people of Israel back to God. He was faithful to obey the call of God on his life.

Read the account in 1 Kings 18:16-39.

Elijah knew God had sent him on this mission, and he trusted that God would be faithful. Elijah may have built the altar, but God constructed the entire plan. Because of his trust in God's faithfulness, Elijah obediently followed the plan, and the result was the people confessing that the Lord is the one true God.

What does Elijah's story teach you about your role in evangelism?

What obstacles stand to threaten your faithfulness?

How has God displayed His faithfulness in your life despite obstacles?

Then the LORD's fire fell and consumed the burnt offering, the wood, the stones, and the dust, and it licked up the water that was in the trench. When all the people saw it, they fell facedown and said, "The LORD, he is God! The LORD, he is God!"
1 Kings 18:38-39

How does God's *past* faithfulness shape your *current* faithfulness?

Later in this book, we will talk about boldness. There's no doubt that boldness is a key part of evangelism. Elijah was bold in his interactions with the false prophets. He had seen God provide for him in the past, and he trusted God to show up in the future. He knew God would not fail. Reminding ourselves of the ways God has been faithful in the past helps us trust that He will continue to be faithful as we obediently step out to share the gospel.

Write down at least five times you have seen God show up in your life. Pray and thank Him for His faithfulness. Ask Him to help you remember His faithfulness as you seek to be faithful in obedience.

PERSONAL DAY 2

Faithful in Love

The last supper was full of surprises, but one of the most unexpected was the moment Jesus knelt to wash His disciples' feet. There are a couple of reasons why this was such a shocking event. First, imagine how torn up their feet had to have been! They walked in sandals on dusty roads all day, every day, with limited access to water. That's dirt on another level.

Because of this nasty reality, foot-washing was a job reserved for the lowest servant. But the Son of God humbly chose to wash the feet of His friends. Think about who was in the room and what they were about to do. The denier—Peter. The betrayer—Judas. And a bunch of guys who would run scared as soon as things turned for the worse. Jesus knew everything that was going to happen in the coming hours and days, and yet He served each of them willingly.

Even though Jesus knew what was to come with His disciples, He didn't leave any of them out. Washing their feet was a perfect foreshadowing of what He would soon do on the cross—die for those who had sent Him to His death.

How does it make you feel when you think about what Jesus did for His disciples, even though He knew how they were about to fail Him and what was about to happen to Him on the cross?

We are called to live like Jesus. In evangelism, that means faithfully proclaiming the gospel to those who don't agree with us. It means loving people who might reject or insult us. Jesus did this all the time! He loyally loved disciples who left Him high and dry when He needed them most. He preached to crowds that walked away from Him. He continued to engage with the Pharisees even though they questioned and plotted against Him. He persevered in sacrificial love because the difficulties were worth it—He got through to some of them! Some of the early Christians were Pharisees (Acts 15). Nicodemus was one of them (John 3). And Paul, maybe the most famous Pharisee of all, became arguably the greatest Christian missionary in history.

So what's the point? We love people because we are called to. All people need the gospel and we don't have the ability to tell whose heart is open to the gospel and whose is not. But no matter where we go or who we encounter, we operate in love. We faithfully serve people. Because even if people seem like they will be unreceptive, we are planting and watering seeds with our words and our witness.

What are some specific ways you can operate with love? List three below.

1.

2.

3.

Why is love necessary in an evangelistic conversation?

It's worth noting that being faithful in love does not mean just a moment of service. We need to be faithful long-term and be expectant for what God will do.

Read John 9:1-38.

Jesus not only gave the blind man sight, but He also kept tabs on the man and returned to him later. After the Pharisees questioned the man about his healing, they threw him out of the synagogue. That's when Jesus arrived back on the scene. Jesus had served this man and shown him love, and after the fact, as He continued to interact with him, the blind man was ready to receive salvation. "Do you believe in the Son of Man?" Jesus asked him. He responds with a ready heart, "Who is he, Sir, that I may believe in him?" (John 9:35-36).

As soon as Jesus told him, "That would be me," the man instantly fell at Jesus's feet and worshiped Him. By meeting the man's physical needs out of love, Jesus prepared his heart to be receptive to the fact that He was the Messiah.

What material or physical needs can you meet for someone this week?

How can these opportunities lead to gospel conversations?

Who have you given up on in the past? In what way can you re-engage with this person and serve him or her in love?

Another way to be faithful in loving people is by listening to their stories. Sometimes, we jump the gun and give our whole gospel presentation before we even know who we're talking to. Instead of telling people we want to talk to them about God, we can ask questions like, "What do you think about God?" or "Who is Jesus to you?" Ask them where they find comfort when they experience pain or grief. Actually find out who they are. Not only do questions like this help lower the risk of rejection, they help people feel seen and valued. When we affirm their value in Jesus, their hearts will be more open to His love and grace.

Think about the last person you talked with about Jesus. How much do you know about this individual?

How can you follow up this week to continue to learn more about that person?

Pray and ask God to help you be faithful in love and obedience as you step out to share His love with others.

PERSONAL DAY 3

Evangelistic Exercise

It's time to practice faithfulness in your relationships through service and love.

Who has God put on your heart this week to seek out and engage in a gospel conversation?

What needs does that person have that you can help meet this week? What steps do you need to take to make that happen?

How can this act of love and service potentially create fertile ground for a gospel conversation?

How will you continue to be faithful in this relationship beyond this initial act of service?

What are some ways you can invite this person into your life in a more significant way?

After you serve this person this week, return to this page and record how the interaction went in the space below. Take notes on things he or she said to reference in future conversations. What will you do next to continue to pour into this relationship?

Week 4

WIN HEARTS

Group Time

START

Welcome to week 4 of **Everyday Evangelism**. *Briefly discuss the last session and talk about any questions students may have.*

Icebreaker: Ask for two volunteers to play a game. Think of a common, everyday occupation like firefighter or nurse. Then ask one of the students, "How many guesses will it take you to figure out what job I'm thinking of?" If the student says "seven," ask the second student if he or she can guess it in six. If the second student thinks he or she can, let that student begin guessing. By asking yes or no questions, the second student has six guesses to figure out what job you're thinking of. If the student can get it in six guesses, the second student wins. If not, the first student gets to ask one more question. If the first student gets it, he or she wins.

In our time together so far, we have emphasized the importance of love in evangelism. We tend to associate evangelism and apologetics with arguments, but arguments aren't what attract people to Jesus. Our goal in evangelism isn't to win arguments—it's to win hearts. So how do we do that effectively? We have to recognize what is and is not our job.

> *For the word of God is living and effective and sharper than any double-edged sword, penetrating as far as the separation of soul and spirit, joints and marrow. It is able to judge the thoughts and intentions of the heart.*
> **HEBREWS 4:12**

God's Word brings people to the truth of the gospel, out of the darkness and into the light. Our job is to present the truth in a way that the gospel itself is the only stumbling block. If we faithfully deliver the Word, it will effectively address the hearts of the people we interact with.

As Christians, we often believe the world is rejecting the gospel. But what if that's not always the case? What if they're rejecting the way it was delivered? How we give the gospel to others matters. We never want our tone or behavior to be the reason someone rejects the gospel.

Pray that God would soften your heart for the lost while giving you a passion for His truth.

WATCH

Use this page to take notes and fill in the blanks as you watch video session 4.

1. When you tell someone about Jesus, you are an __________________. But the moment they start asking you questions, you are an ____________________.

2. ____________ are you doing this? Are you doing this to look smart? Intelligent? Or because of pride? Or are you doing this because of _____________?

3. "If we pay attention how God wants us to treat ____________, it's not just because it reflects His _______________________, it's the most effective way."

4. "Even though we fundamentally disagreed on theology, we became _______________ and I think that's how we should do _________________ like real life."

5. "If I'm looking to win an _________________ and not a _____________, I'm already starting on bad ground."

"I don't think I was ever trying to win his heart. I was always trying to win an argument."

To access the teaching sessions, use the instructions in the back of your Bible study book.

DISCUSS

Use this page to facilitate the group discussion.

1. **Share about a time someone had to tell you difficult news. How was that news delivered?**

2. **How did the way the news was delivered impact the way you received it (positively or negatively)?**

No matter what news was shared with you, a kind and calm presentation is received better than an abrasive one. The truth is often hard to hear. People sometimes respond with defensiveness when you try to bring up the gospel. Nobody likes to entertain the possibility that his or her worldview is wrong. So how do we share this difficult news? We approach with kindness. Evangelism is never strictly intellectual. To win hearts for Jesus, we have to actually care about people's hearts!

3. **Do you remember the first time you were presented the gospel? If so, how did you respond? If not, how about the first time you shared the gospel with someone? How was it received?**

4. **If you had a negative experience for either of these situations, what could have happened differently that would have made it better received?**

Even when we approach people with gentleness, they may sometimes still be combative in response. What do we do in that situation?

> *A gentle answer turns away anger, but a harsh word stirs up wrath.*
> **PROVERBS 15:1**

Human nature causes us to treat people the way we are treated. If someone is rude to us, we usually respond rudely. It's much easier to be kind to people who are kind to us. But if we are in Christ, we have a new nature. We are no longer bound by our sin nature; instead, we are free to live by Jesus's example. We have to reject the impulse to get defensive or argue in a hostile and mean-spirited way. If we continue to respond gently, it can change the entire trajectory of the interaction.

Read Colossians 3:1-15.

5. **What are the differences between your old earthly nature and the new nature you've been given in Christ?**

6. **What characteristics do you need to remember to "put on" (vv. 12-14) daily? How do these things help in evangelism?**

Putting on the new self is something we have to practice. It will become more and more natural for us as we lean on the Holy Spirit, but it is an active choice to live with the new nature Jesus has given us. Keep this in mind in every evangelistic conversation. Ask the Spirit to bear fruit in you as you interact with those who need His truth.

Read Galatians 5:22-23.

7. **Walk through the fruit of the Spirit and discuss how each one can help as you give the gospel to others.**

God isn't commissioning us to be argumentative. He's commissioning us to be effective. The people who may appear opposed to the gospel aren't really opponents. We were once in the very same position as the lost people we encounter. If it wasn't for Jesus, we would still be that way. Jesus took on our punishment so we could be made right with God. Our Good Shepherd came looking for us, gathered us up, and brought us back into the flock. He didn't do that with an iron fist or cattle prod. He brought us back to Himself with tenderness and humility. And now we go and do the same, as the Shepherd's ambassadors, with compassion, gentleness, and unshakable love.

Use this time to pray for one another as you close your time together.

PRAYER REQUESTS

"Therefore, as God's chosen
ones, holy and dearly
loved, put on compassion,
kindness, humility,
gentleness, and patience,
bearing with one another
and forgiving one another
if anyone has a grievance
against another. Just
as the Lord has forgiven
you, so you are also to
forgive. Above all, put
on love, which is the
perfect bond of unity."

COLOSSIANS 3:12-14

Week 4 Win Hearts

PERSONAL DAY 1

Through Behavior and Words

> *Finally, all of you be like-minded and sympathetic, love one another, and be compassionate and humble, not paying back evil for evil or insult for insult but, on the contrary, giving a blessing, since you were called for this, so that you may inherit a blessing.*
> **1 PETER 3:8-9**

These verses are written to churches that had been dispersed abroad (see 1 Peter 1:1). These believers had been through the wringer—persecuted and exiled for their faith in Jesus—and Peter still instructed them to move through life in love. If you really think about what they must have experienced as they were rejected from their hometowns and displaced, it seems like it would be almost impossible to wake up and put on love every day. But remember, they had a new nature. In their old sin nature, they probably would have stewed in anger, retaliated, and lived with hard, bitter hearts. But because the Spirit of God was living in them, they were empowered to overcome natural responses and operate in love, regardless of the difficulties they experienced.

Think about how compelling their kindness, peacefulness, and positivity must have been to the people around them witnessing them living with joy despite difficult circumstances. Walking in our new nature in the face of persecution will open doors for us to have powerful conversations about Jesus with those who need Him. They will see His power to sustain us and make us new in real time.

What has to happen in our hearts so that love is our first response?

Why should we treat nonbelievers with love and respect? What does that show them about Jesus?

Paul also had a lot to say to the early church about how they were to act toward others. Colossae was a diverse city, full of competing belief systems just like in our society. In Colossians 4:2-6, Paul encourages them:

> *Devote yourselves to prayer; stay alert in it with thanksgiving. At the same time, pray also for us that God may open a door to us for the word, to speak the mystery of Christ, for which I am in chains, so that I may make it known as I should. Act wisely toward outsiders, making the most of the time. Let your speech always be gracious, seasoned with salt, so that you may know how you should answer each person.*

Paul first reminds the church to pray diligently, thanking God for what He is doing and asking Him to create opportunities for more to come to faith in Jesus. We should consistently ask God to open doors for us to share the gospel. We should lift others up by name and ask God to rescue them from sin. As we spend time with God in prayer, He will give us an even greater heart to see people come to know Him. He will empty us of ourselves—of our old nature, our fear, our hesitations—and fill us with more of Himself. We can never discount the role of prayer in our evangelism. God listens when we pray!

What does your prayer life look like currently? How might your outlook change if you focused your prayers on others and their needs more than your own?

Make a list of people you know who are far from God. Commit to praying for them daily this week. Write their names below. Come back to this list often to be reminded of these people.

Paul goes on with specific instructions for how we should tell the truth to outsiders in order to win hearts (see Col. 4:5-6). He says we should act wisely and that our speech should be full of grace and "seasoned with salt." Let's look at each of these three ideas.

First, wisdom. When we are wise in evangelism, we carefully measure our words and make sure that we do not speak thoughtlessly or recklessly. We consider who we are talking to before we talk and act accordingly.

Have you had a conversation lately where you lacked wisdom?
How can you be more wise in the future?

Secondly, Paul says we need to be full of grace. We should give unmerited favor to others because that's what Jesus did for us. That means we let things go. We forgive. And we give without the expectation to receive.

Lastly, Paul says we should have words that are like salt. When it is used properly, salt brings out the flavors of food and makes everything better. When we speak, our words should be delivered with the best of flavors. The things we say should make the people around us better.

How can you infuse your speech with salt? How can you see and call out the best in others as a way of speaking life to them and building a relationship?

PERSONAL DAY 2

Through Spiritual Growth

If you find it hard to speak the truth in love, you aren't alone. The whole idea goes against our nature, especially when we're met with opposition or indifference. It takes time for all of us to consistently walk in our new nature. We have to put on the new self daily (see Eph. 4:24). As our relationship with Jesus grows, this posture becomes more natural to us than our sinful nature.

Jesus is a Good Shepherd. He doesn't bring us into the flock for us to live as lambs our whole lives. He wants to help us grow. As He tends to us, we grow and mature. We get stronger. We become wiser. We can handle more difficult situations. But we have to stay close to Jesus. Proximity to the Shepherd is what empowers the growth of the sheep. If we want to grow in our speech, we have to grow in our hearts.

> *"A good tree doesn't produce bad fruit; on the other hand, a bad tree doesn't produce good fruit. For each tree is known by its own fruit. Figs aren't gathered from thornbushes, or grapes picked from a bramble bush. A good person produces good out of the good stored up in his heart. An evil person produces evil out of the evil stored up in his heart, for his mouth speaks from the overflow of the heart."*
> **LUKE 6:43-45**

We can't produce life-giving words if we aren't growing in Jesus. Whatever is going on in our hearts will come out of our mouths. So the question is, what are we doing to grow?

How would you describe the current condition of your heart? What impacts your heart the most right now?

In what ways do you pursue God daily?

We should continually be learning about God and ourselves through the Scriptures. What's one thing you've learned about God recently?

If there is something apart from God that currently has your heart, consider fasting from it. Anything that has our attention more than God is an idol. It could be something that isn't bad in and of itself but has improper priority in our lives. Fasting is a great way to reorder our attention. It removes the thing that takes our attention off of God, allowing us to refocus on Him. Fill the time you were spending on this distraction with prayer, worship, reading the Bible, and friendships that point you to Jesus. Growth can be painful at times, but it is necessary.

> *"Why do you call me 'Lord, Lord,' and don't do the things I say? I will show you what someone is like who comes to me, hears my words, and acts on them: He is like a man building a house, who dug deep and laid the foundation on the rock. When the flood came, the river crashed against that house and couldn't shake it, because it was well built."*
> **LUKE 6:46-48**

As we spend time with Jesus learning from His Word, we lay a foundation that cannot be shaken. We build a faith full of strength and confidence that does not have to revert to defensiveness or arguments when we face opposition. We become resilient, and that resilience translates to perseverance in love. Closeness with Jesus empowers us to evangelize in a way that wins hearts.

One of the best gifts God has given us in the church is community to help us in our journey to grow. You don't have to do this alone! In fact, you shouldn't. If you go to the gym to strength train with heavy weights, you need a spotter. Your spotter makes sure your technique is safe. He or she encourages you to push yourself and keep getting stronger.

And he or she makes sure you actually show up day after day! Partnership makes the difficult parts of growing more fun and helps us persevere. You need a spiritual growth partner. It may be a best friend, a mentor, or a group of like-minded believers. You'll find your spiritual growth will happen on a greater scale when you aren't the only one putting in the work.

> *"But the one who hears and does not act is like a man who built a house on the ground without a foundation. The river crashed against it, and immediately it collapsed. And the destruction of that house was great."*
> **LUKE 6:49**

How does a lack of perseverance in your spiritual growth impact your evangelism?

Is God's Word the foundation for your life? Why or why not?

Who in your life can help evaluate your obedience and hold you accountable as you grow? How can you partner with him or her this week?

PERSONAL DAY 3

Evangelistic Exercise

In order to give the gospel in a way that wins hearts, you have to have a healthy heart and a strong foundation built on closeness with Jesus. Before you take your next step in reaching out to others, take stock of the current condition of your heart and identify growth areas. Make a plan to consistently grow in your spiritual life as you move forward in your call to evangelism.

Think about how you speak to and act toward others (including your parents, teachers, friends, etc.). What does the way you treat them with your words and actions reveal about the condition of your heart?

In what ways do you need God to transform your heart?

How often do you spend time with Jesus? What does that time look like?

In what ways do you need to grow in your faith? Why do you think these specific areas of growth are important?

What are some ways you can be more consistent in your relationship with Jesus?

How will a closer relationship with Jesus impact your evangelism?

What will you do this week to grow spiritually?

When you have a moment of failure in your walk with Jesus, what needs to happen so that you move forward instead of getting stuck in that sin?

What are adjustments you feel you need to make in order to focus more on people's hearts than arguments?

Week 5

KNOW THE TRUTH

Group Time

START

Welcome to week 5 of **Everyday Evangelism**. *Briefly discuss the last session and talk about any questions students may have.*

Jesus's ministry was characterized by telling the truth with compassion for the people He was addressing. He taught the truths of the kingdom with both deep conviction and compassion. We are called to do the same. But in order to share the truth, we need to know the truth.

Icebreaker: On a whiteboard or giant sticky pad, write, "What are the essentials of the gospel?" Record students' responses and discuss why they feel these are essential elements of the gospel.

At this stage in life, your peers are sorting out what they believe about God. The truth is, everyone believes in something—even people who claim to believe in nothing. The people you encounter will all have some way that they view the world, humanity, and God. The options for how people believe are almost endless: they may belong to another religion, be vaguely spiritual, believe everyone goes to heaven, be an agnostic, have no religious beliefs at all, or they may even firmly believe that there is no God or spiritual realm. But they have a belief system. Each of these worldviews carry different questions and hesitations about Christianity. If we can learn and know the truth about the gospel, we will be able to interact with people of all different beliefs with confidence and love.

Pray that God would build you up so that you can answer genuine questions about the gospel with clarity, compassion, and conviction.

WATCH

Use this page to take notes and fill in the blanks as you watch video session 5.

1. If you don't have a firm ____________________ for what you believe, you can never properly ________________ it.

2. People might ____________ the key foundations and essentials of the gospel but they don't know how to __________ it to the context they live in.

3. Our evangelism and apologetics are supposed to direct us to a ______________—to make _________________ of all nations.

4. Asking questions gives you an opportunity to break down ___________________ about God and His ______________.

5. Asking good questions allows us to ______________ to people effectively.

"Do you mind if I explain what I believe the Bible says the gospel is?"

To access the teaching sessions, use the instructions in the back of your Bible study book.

DISCUSS

Use this page to facilitate the group discussion.

1. **What would you say if someone asked you who Jesus is?**

Read John 3:16-18.

2. **What was God's purpose in sending Jesus into the world?**

3. **Who can be saved?**

4. **How is a person saved?**

You can't communicate the gospel without explaining Jesus and His work on the cross. Thankfully, John 3:16-18 covers much of the gospel message. Without Jesus, we are condemned, or judged, because of our sin. The punishment for our sin is death. But because God loved us, He sent Jesus to die in our place. If we have faith that Jesus is who He says He is and that He is the only way for us to be saved, we will be.

The reason Jesus is the most important point in any discussion about faith is that He brings everybody to a decision. You can say you believe in God all day long, and most religions won't question the existence of a higher power. But once you say, "I believe Jesus is God," you separate yourself from everything else. Those with other belief systems have decided not to believe that Jesus is God.

Let's explore this truth by reading Colossians 1:15-20. (We will come back to these verses again in personal day 1 this week.)

5. **How does Paul describe Jesus in this passage?**

6. **Why is it essential to the gospel that Jesus is God?**

7. **How did Jesus, who created all things, make peace between humanity and God?**

The problem isn't that other religions don't believe Jesus existed. It's that they don't believe He is God. Some believe He was a man—which He was (see John 1:14). Others believe He was a prophet—which He was (see Acts 3:22-23). Some, like Mormons, believe He was God's son—which He is (see Matthew 3:17). Even Jehovah's Witnesses believe He's the way, the truth, and the life—which He is (see John 14:6). The problem is, these religions believe that Jesus was only those things—not all of those things. They deny He is God.

If Jesus is God, it means that He didn't just offer some good teachings that we can decide to follow if we choose. It means He is the Lord, our highest authority, and we owe Him our worship and allegiance. The understanding that Jesus was fully God and fully human is one essential part of what it means to believe in Jesus.

8. Why do we need to explain this gospel essential in evangelistic conversations?

9. What are other essential gospel truths you may need to learn more about in order to feel prepared for evangelism?

Today's conversation is just a starting point. As we step out in faith, there will be other key beliefs we need to understand. But any believer at any stage of spiritual growth can share the gospel with someone because if you know enough to repent and believe in Jesus, you know enough to tell someone what He's done for you.

Use this time to pray for one another as you close your time together.

PRAYER REQUESTS

“For God loved the world in this way: He gave his one and only Son, so that everyone who believes in him will not perish but have eternal life. For God did not send his Son into the world to condemn the world, but to save the world through him. Anyone who believes in him is not condemned, but anyone who does not believe is already condemned, because he has not believed in the name of the one and only Son of God.”

JOHN 3:16-18

Week 5 Know the Truth

PERSONAL DAY 1

Jesus Is God

Understanding what the Bible teaches is important when encountering people from other worldviews and belief systems. Many other systems of belief incorporate pieces of the Bible in their teaching. They might even quote Scripture and use it to try and prove their points. This has always been the case—the devil has always taken God's Word out of context and woven in half-truths (which are whole lies) and confusion into the truth.

What are examples of half-truths in other belief systems that you may have encountered before?

Read Philippians 2:5-11.

Some religions take these verses out of context and claim that here it says Jesus is not equal to God. But Paul was making a specific point when he wrote about Jesus this way. At the beginning of Philippians 2, Paul tells the church, "Do nothing out of selfish ambition or conceit, but in humility consider others as more important than yourselves." He tells them, "Adopt the same attitude as that of Christ Jesus" (Philippians 2:3,5).

Paul's main point in getting the Philippians to think about Jesus emptying Himself "by assuming the form of a servant" (v. 7) is to point them to Jesus's great humility so that they can imitate it. You might be wondering, why is Jesus "not considering equality with God as something to be exploited" (v. 6) an example of great humility? It's because Jesus is God. At no point did Jesus stop being God; He became a human, embracing all its limitations, and became like us so that He could be a suitable sacrifice on the cross (see verse 8).

Let's revisit Colossians 1:15-20. The city of Colossae was relatively small but filled with a mix of cultures, backgrounds, and religions. The belief systems were diverse, just like in our society. The church itself was dealing with some sort of heresy (incorrect teaching) that had infiltrated their theology through false teachers in the church.

Knowing this context, look at how Paul began this letter. To bring the church back to the true gospel, Paul taught on Jesus's identity and nature.

Read Colossians 1:15-20.

What truths about Jesus does Paul explain in these verses?

Why is Jesus's nature crucial to the gospel?

Why would Paul highlight these characteristics of Jesus to a church surrounded by diverse belief systems?

How would you use these verses to explain who Jesus is?

Paul is reminding his audience that Jesus has always existed. He is God, and everything was made through Him. When we say that Jesus is God, we are not saying that Jesus and God the Father are the same Person of the Trinity. What we are saying is that Jesus, the Father, and the Holy Spirit share the same essence. They all are equally God, coexisting as three distinct but coequal Persons of the Trinity.

That's a lot to take in, right? But that's why this topic comes up in so many apologetic conversations. It's easy to get all twisted up. Some religions (like Jehovah's Witnesses and Mormons) believe Jesus is the son of God, but they deny that He has always existed.

It's important to understand that God doesn't exist in the same way we humans do. Therefore, our comparisons and analogies may not accurately represent who God is. For instance, some people try to use water as a way to explain the Trinity. Water can exist as a liquid, a solid, or a vapor. However, this analogy falls short because a single water molecule cannot exist as liquid, solid, and vapor at the same time. In a divinely mysterious way, God exists, and has always existed, as Father, Son, and Holy Spirit—one God in being, expressed as three co-equal Persons at the same time.

If Jesus isn't God, His death on the cross was for nothing, and we shouldn't follow Him. But Jesus is God, which changes everything.

It's possible the people you are around and likely to have gospel conversations with aren't talking about God on this level. Their concerns about the Christian faith might focus on other aspects.

What issues do people around you have with Christianity?

How would you answer their concerns? If you aren't sure, do some research to find Scriptures that point them back to the truth. Write their questions/ issues below along with Scripture references that answer them. Be sure to look at the context of these Scripture references as well to grasp the full picture of the truths you are explaining.

PERSONAL DAY 2

We Are Saved by Grace

Another essential to our faith is how we are saved. Every religion has a way to salvation, and virtually every religion in the world teaches that we have to work to please God and earn our salvation. Jews believe they must adhere to a lengthy list of laws and customs to please God. Muslims believe they must pray five times a day, fast, give to the poor, pledge allegiance to Muhammad, and make a pilgrimage to Mecca. The Latter-day Saints' (Mormons) faith says that works are needed to be saved. Hindus believe they must purify themselves. And Buddhists believe they must renounce all worldly things and die to self to achieve nirvana.

Christianity stands alone in that we believe salvation isn't something we can earn or achieve. It's impossible. That is why Jesus came to do the work for us.

Read Ephesians 2:8-9.

How would you summarize these verses in your own words?

Why is it difficult for even Bible-believing Christians to trust that they are saved by grace through faith?

How does Jesus finishing the work on the cross (instead of us having to work for it) give people the confidence to know if they are saved or not?

Read Romans 10:9-10.

How is someone saved?

Read James 2:17.

Often, those who believe we are saved by our works look at James 2:17 as proof of their position. Again, we have to look at the context to determine what this verse means. James isn't saying that works save us but rather that genuine faith will be observable in the fruit of our lives.

Set aside James for a moment and read Romans 4:4-8 and Luke 7:36-50.

These verses (and there are many more) make it clear that faith alone is what saves. We trust Jesus alone for salvation so that we can't boast that we did it on our own. So how should we view what James said? Our faith leads us to obedience, which is the fruit of our salvation. Our works are not what make us right (justified) in the eyes of God; they're evidence that we have been justified. Our works are an outpouring of the grace we've received. This doesn't mean that if we don't work, our faith dies. It means that if our lives don't have evidence of good works, we probably never had faith to begin with. Our works are visible fruit of the faith within us.

What good works has God been producing within you?

If you were asked, how would you explain to someone the difference between the gospel and a salvation based on our works?

Read Ephesians 2:1-5.

Paul says it plainly: we were dead in our sins (v. 1). Dead people cannot work toward salvation. But because He loved us, God showed us mercy and made us alive in Jesus (vv. 4-5). There's nothing we could possibly do to deserve this grace. It is the unmerited favor of God that He gives us through faith.

Even if we weren't dead in our sins, our works would just never be enough to earn salvation. The only appropriate payment for our sin is death. We can't pay that debt ourselves. Jesus sacrificed Himself for us so that if we believe in Him, we can be rescued. He died in our place. When we trust in Jesus, we are saved by God's grace.

Why is the grace of God good news?

PERSONAL DAY 3

Evangelistic Exercise

In my context, I often encounter Hebrew Israelites, Mormons, Muslims, and Jehovah's Witnesses. In order to have effective conversations with them, I needed to know the basics of what they believe and their general views of Christianity. It took time, lots of interactions, and intentional research, but I was able to gather that essential information and go into conversations prepared. You need to be able to do the same.

Which three belief systems (other than Christianity) do you encounter most?

For those three religions or belief systems, research the following: salvation path, similarities to Christianity, differences from Christianity, and conflicts with Christianity.

In a journal, take notes that summarize some of these points. Then, research and find Scripture that you can use to direct people to the truth. Be sure to check the context of Scripture in order to communicate the truth clearly. Record the Scripture references below your summary. (Refer to the example on the following page.)

The goal of this exercise is to be prepared to support the truth, especially against specific arguments and viewpoints from belief systems you often encounter. In the next session, we learn more about how to present the truth that has saved and changed our lives.

EXAMPLE:

Religion: Islam

Path to Salvation: Worshiping God alone through the Five Pillars of Islam:

- Declaration of faith to Allah (God)
- Prayer
- Almsgiving (donation to charity)
- Fasting
- Pilgrimage to Mecca

Faith in Allah is faith in a god claimed to be Moses's God (with no other persons), but they are not the same because Moses's God is three in one.

Similarities to Christianity:

- "Belief" in the Bible (when not in conflict with the Quran)
- Belief in the "God" of Abraham—however, viewing God the Father as the only god means Allah ("God") is not the true God

Differences:

- Salvation path
- Different inspired scriptures (Quran vs. Bible)
- Jesus was simply a prophet
- Original forgiveness instead of original sin

Conflicts:

- Quran supersedes the Bible
- Works-based salvation
- Muhammad supersedes Jesus
- Believes Jesus's "message" but doesn't believe He is God

Verses to address these differences and conflicts: John 3:16-17 (with Luke 10:16; John 6:45; John 14:6); 1 John 2:23; 1 Timothy 2:5; John 5:23; 2 Timothy 3:16-17; Romans 3:23; Revelation 22:18-19.

Week 6

BE BOLD

Group Time

START

Welcome to week 6 of **Everyday Evangelism**. *Briefly discuss the last session and talk about any questions students may have.*

Icebreaker: Ask students to find a picture in their phone's photo library that they feel sums up who they are. If a student doesn't have a phone, he or she can share a story instead. Allow each student in the group to share his or her picture or story. If the group is larger, direct students to get into smaller groups of three to five students to share their pictures or stories.

Now that you have been equipped with the right heart and understanding to have effective gospel conversations, it's time to step out into evangelism. Hopefully, you feel much more confident about going out and sharing the truth that brought you from darkness into light. If you're still feeling hesitant in some ways, that's okay—but it's time to be bold. When people think of boldness, they usually picture a strong warrior type of person—someone waving a sword and ready to storm the battlefield. But boldness is simply being faithful to what God has asked you to do.

A moment ago we shared pictures or stories that summarize who we are. We are all created uniquely and that is by God's design. Because He made you unique, you can share the gospel unlike anyone else in the world. Recognizing the unique way God has created you to represent the gospel is essential to your effectiveness as an evangelist. If you try to put on a persona that you think an evangelist should have, people will pick up on that insincerity. So take a look at how God made you, the gifts He's given you, and how that design can be used by Jesus. God isn't expecting you to become someone else. He's expecting you to be obedient to love people and share Jesus in that unique way He's given you. Boldness comes from trusting His design and His presence within you.

> *For we are his workmanship, created in Christ Jesus for good works, which God prepared ahead of time for us to do.*
> **EPHESIANS 2:10**

Pray that God would use your experience in this book to make you bold.

WATCH

Use this page to take notes and fill in the blanks as you watch video session 6.

1. "I believe that God is going to _______ people how He has ____________ made them."

2. How can you be __________ in how He has uniquely made you?

3. "When the Lord put an opportunity in her _______, she didn't say _______."

4. We have to be ready to say _______ and be ________________ to the Lord when the time calls for it.

5. In order for the ______________ to be the body (of Christ), we have to not make ________________________ look the same.

"Boldness is more about obedience to God than being fearless before men."

To access the teaching sessions, use the instructions in the back of your Bible study book.

DISCUSS

Use this page to facilitate the group discussion.

1. **God uses people as He has uniquely made them. How does this challenge your understanding of what it means to be bold?**

2. **What are some of the specific traits and strengths God has given you?**

Whether you were created to be a street evangelist or have a more subtle approach to evangelism, sharing the gospel is going to require boldness. And the reality is, it's hard to be bold in today's culture where truth is considered relative and everyone is allowed to define his or her own existence. But if we don't cultivate courage and obediently speak the truth, the people around us will stay lost in darkness. The world needs to know the truth that the Creator God is the only One who defines our existence and we can only experience true life in Him.

Read 1 Corinthians 12:12-20.

3. **Why is seeing the church as a body with many parts and gifts freeing for us in our evangelism?**

4. **Why is one approach to evangelism not inherently "better" than another?**

God has not made all of us the same. Each of has gifts that He has given to build His kingdom. All of us are called to share the gospel, but how we do it will look different because we all have different gifts. God may have wired you to have conversations with the person you just met at the movie theater, or He might have wired you to develop relationships with the people you eat lunch with everyday and share the gospel as those relationships deepen. Either way, we can be certain that God plans to use all of us with His Spirit working through us to take the gospel into our communities and to the world.

5. **When have you felt a sense of guilt surrounding evangelism? How has this session helped you think differently about that?**

6. **Discuss this statement: "Boldness is more about being obedient to God than it is being fearless before men." How does this help you think differently about boldness?**

7. **Based on this definition of boldness, how can you grow in boldness?**

As we grow as evangelists, we can have a tendency to burden ourselves in a way that the Lord isn't burdening us. We feel like our evangelism has to look a certain way, but that simply isn't the case. One of the goals of this book is to help you see that everyone can be an evangelist by tapping into the way that God has uniquely made each person. God has gifted you to share the gospel in a specific way. You will discover what that way is by being bold enough to step out and share.

8. **Where is God leading you to be bold? Express this out loud to the group so your friends can hold you accountable.**

9. **What is your biggest takeaway from these six sessions? Close your time together by praying for each other in your unique callings.**

Use this time to pray for one another as you close your time together.

PRAYER REQUESTS

"For just as the body is one and has many parts, and all the parts of that body, though many, are one body—so also is Christ."

1 CORINTHIANS 12:12

Week 6 Be Bold

PERSONAL DAY 1

Regardless of the Outcome

Boldness is more about being obedient to God than fearless before people. But sometimes boldness and obedience will lead to rejection. In those moments, we need to trust God and embrace the fact that we are being obedient to His call. We never know how our bold steps will be taken by those we are walking towards. If we already knew what the result would be, it wouldn't be boldness. Throughout Scripture, we see moments when regular people, filled with the Holy Spirit, stood up for their faith and changed lives. At other times, their boldness was rejected because of their faith in Jesus.

Jesus tells us in John 15 that persecution is inevitable. In verses 18-19, He says, "If the world hates you, understand that it hated me before it hated you. If you were of the world, the world would love you as its own. However, because you are not of the world, but I have chosen you out of it, the world hates you." Jesus is essentially saying, "If you live for me and tell the truth to the world around you, they will not like it. Because you know and follow me, you will live differently than the world does. And if you are different, they will hate you." But Jesus also encourages us with the reality that they hated Him, too. If the world treats you like they treated the Son of God, it's safe to say you're in good company.

How are Jesus's words comforting as you seek to share the gospel?

When has fear kept you from being bold? What did you learn from that experience?

When was the last time you boldly obeyed the Lord? How did it turn out?

Why must we always evaluate our boldness on our obedience rather than our inward feelings or people's response?

Jesus warned us that the world would hate us, but there's a way to continue to be bold even when the world pushes back. We have to remember we are never alone in our evangelistic efforts. God is always with us, willing and able to empower us to persevere. We just have to stay connected to the Source of our power.

Look at the beginning of John 15. It's no accident that Jesus used the analogy of the vine and the branches right before His prediction of persecution. He reminded the disciples that as long as they stayed connected to Him, their efforts to love and serve and share the gospel would be powerful and effective. Boldness flows through our connection to Him.

> *"If you remain in me and my words remain in you, ask whatever you want and it will be done for you. My Father is glorified by this: that you produce much fruit and prove to be my disciples."*
> **JOHN 15:7-8**

Jesus cautioned, "You can do nothing without me" (v. 5). Our boldness only makes a difference when we are connected to Jesus. To persevere and thrive as branches, we have to stay connected to the vine through reading the Word, prayer, and daily obedience to the Holy Spirit. Part of being obedient to God is daily taking that time to nurture our connection to the vine so that we know what God wants us to do. We understand from the Spirit and the Word where He's leading us and make ourselves sensitive and receptive to His call in our lives.

How would you describe your current connection with God? Can you see a connection between that relationship and your current level of boldness?

In what ways can you more consistently connect with God?

Jesus promises to sustain us and empower us to bear fruit if we remain in Him. In Matthew 5, Jesus gives additional encouragement for Christians who endure persecution because of the gospel. God will not only sustain us and receive glory as we share the truth, but we will also be blessed even as the world hates us.

> *"Blessed are those who are persecuted because of righteousness, for the kingdom of heaven is theirs. You are blessed when they insult you and persecute you and falsely say every kind of evil against you because of me. Be glad and rejoice, because your reward is great in heaven. For that is how they persecuted the prophets who were before you."*
> **MATTHEW 5:10-12**

Throughout this book, we've talked about how our apologetics can never be motivated by a desire to appear important or impressive. Nothing we do in the realm of evangelism is about us; this calling is all about bringing people into a saving relationship with Jesus for all of eternity. When we walk in evangelism, we live with our eyes on heaven. We aren't worried about earning blessings or rewards here. The blessings of a life lived boldly for Jesus are eternal.

PERSONAL DAY 2

With the Resources God's Given You

You may not think of Joseph of Arimathea often. However, his part in Jesus's story is recorded in all four Gospel accounts, which means he played an important role. The four accounts provide different details:

- Matthew tells us that Joseph was rich (Matthew 27:57).
- Mark tells us that he was a prominent member of the Sanhedrin (Mark 15:43).
- Luke tells us that he was "a good and righteous man . . . who had not agreed with [the Sanhedrin's] plan and action" and that he "was looking forward to the kingdom of God" (Luke 23:50-51).
- John tells us that up until the crucifixion, Joseph had kept his allegiance to Jesus a secret because he had feared retribution by the Sanhedrin (John 19:38).

In the past, what has caused you to be quiet about your faith?

Joseph's fear of how the Sanhedrin would respond to his devotion to Jesus wasn't unfounded—after all, they killed Jesus. But in the crucial moments after Jesus's death, we see Joseph step out of his fear, out of the shadows, into the light of truth. He boldly went to Pilate and asked his permission to bury Jesus's body in a brand-new tomb he had cut from rock. Burying the body of Jesus may not seem like a particularly brave thing to do, but this action sent a loud and clear message to all the Jews that Joseph was on Jesus's side.

The most dangerous time to follow Jesus was not when He was alive; it was after He had been crucified—after He was condemned as a criminal, a blasphemer, and a false prophet. When Jesus gave up His spirit and the sky turned dark, it became a scary time for those who followed Him—which is why the disciples went into hiding after the crucifixion.

Think about that for a second. All of the disciples—His best friends who had followed Him in public for three years—ran away and hid. With the exception of John, they didn't even show up at His crucifixion. But after Jesus was killed, a secret follower named Joseph of Arimathea could not hold in his secret anymore. When the Romans executed people on crosses, the bodies were usually left on the crosses to rot as a warning to other would-be rebels. But Joseph believed Jesus was the Son of God. He was unwilling to let the body of his Lord be treated so disrespectfully. So he acted quickly to make sure Jesus's body would be buried before the Sabbath began. Out of all of Jesus's followers, Joseph was the one took the boldest action after His death. He literally risked his life to make sure that Jesus had a proper Jewish burial.

In what ways do Christians today tend to hide instead of showing boldness?

It's true that during Jesus's life, Joseph's discipleship to Jesus was hushed and hidden. But God gave him the boldness to stand up for his faith when it could cost him the most. As a member of the Sanhedrin, by aligning with Jesus, he risked his fortune, he risked his social status, he risked his position, and he risked his reputation. Taking that bold step in those scary hours risked his very life. He was willing to put it all on the line for his Savior.

In what ways can boldness be dangerous for Christians in today's culture? What current issues are the most treacherous?

Joseph's story should be an encouragement to those who think they're just "not bold." His story shows us that boldness is not a personality trait; rather, it is the willingness to act when God is calling you to. Joseph didn't proclaim his faith in Jesus as a street evangelist; he used the resources God had given him to honor Jesus when there was an opportunity. In doing so, he testified about his faith in a way that was undeniable.

What would it look like for you to use your God-given gifts and resources in the way God has created you to use them?

How can you do this with boldness?

If we are going to be faithful evangelists in a world that condemned Jesus, we have to know that they will come for us, too. Yet even when they do, we can be confident that, as Paul writes in Romans 8, "neither death nor life, nor angels nor rulers, nor things present nor things to come, nor powers, nor height nor depth, nor any other created thing will be able to separate us from the love of God that is in Christ Jesus our Lord" (vv. 38-39). God will always be with you, and He will give you everything you need to walk in boldness and persevere for the sake of the gospel. Stay connected to Jesus. Let His love for people fill your heart and be your motivation. Know the truth, and tell it wherever you go. Share Jesus with the world, and win hearts for His glory.

PERSONAL DAY 3

Evangelistic Exercise

For the final moment of this Bible study, reflect briefly on your biggest takeaways so you can implement what you've learned as you step out boldly in evangelism.

Look back over all the evangelistic exercises from previous sessions. What do you want to remember from these experiences as you share the gospel in the future?

What is the most important thing you want to communicate with people when you share the gospel?

How do you plan to help people understand that you love and care about them as you share the gospel with them?

What is the most likely opposition you'll face in evangelistic conversations in your community? How do you plan to handle that opposition?

How will you remain connected to Jesus moving forward? How do you plan to prepare your heart for evangelistic conversations daily?

Notice that the last three questions all included the word *plan*. You have put in a lot of work throughout this book to prepare to effectively share the gospel, and now, you're ready. You have a plan. It's time to go out and do it!

Look at your schedule and identify a specific time this week when you will have an evangelistic conversation with someone you know or with a stranger. Begin praying for that person now, asking God to prepare his or her heart to receive Him. Ask God to take away any impatience, self-focus, or fear that might hinder you. Then, go out there with a heart full of love and tell the truth.

NOTES

NOTES

NOTES

NOTES

NOTES

NOTES

NOTES

NOTES

Get the most from your study.

Customize your Bible study time with a guided experience.

Can anyone be an evangelist?

Most Christians know we are called to share the gospel, but many of us hesitate for a variety of reasons. We worry about how the message will be received. We're scared of rejections. We're afraid we won't be able to answer questions. Maybe we don't even know how to start the conversation. But the truth is, we're overthinking it. If you love Jesus and have a heart for people to know Him, you have what you need to be an evangelist.

Evangelism isn't about having a systematic process for sharing the gospel. It's not about being able to answer every question about the Bible. It's about love—having the heart of God for His people. When you care about people, meet them where they are, and show them dignity and respect, the door will be open for you to share the truth in a way that can change their lives forever.

In this study, you'll:

- Learn foundational principles of effective evangelism.
- Develop a desire to win hearts instead of arguments.
- Grow in your confidence to explain the essentials of the gospel.
- Find the boldness you need to fulfill the calling of an evangelist.

Lifeway designs trustworthy experiences that fuel ministry. Today, the ministries of Lifeway reach more than 160 countries around the globe. For more information about Lifeway Students, visit lifeway.com/students.

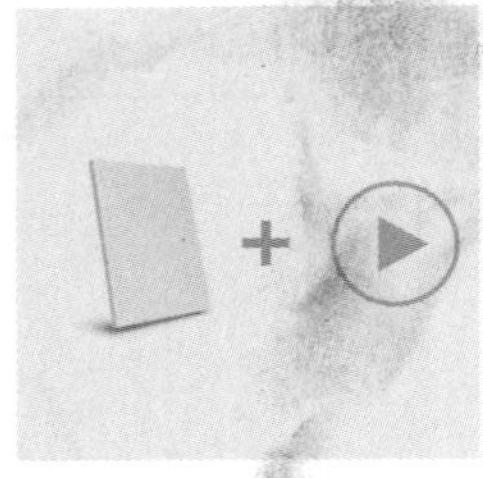

ADDITIONAL RESOURCES

EVERYDAY EVANGELISM
A 6-session Bible study for adults by Preston Perry, including video access

Browse study formats, a free session sample, video clips, church promotional materials, and more at **lifeway.com/everydayevangelism.**